MEZZANINE

MEZZANINE

Poems

ZOË HITZIG

ecco

An Imprint of HarperCollins*Publishers*

HarperCollins books may be purchased for educational, business, or sales promotional use. For information, please email the Special Markets Department at SPsales@harpercollins.com.

Ecco® and HarperCollins® are trademarks of HarperCollins Publishers.

A hardcover edition of this book was published in 2020 by Ecco, an imprint of HarperCollins Publishers.

An extension of this copyright appears on page 85.

Grateful acknowledgment is made for permission to reprint from *The Death of Nature*, by Carolyn Merchant. Used by permission of HarperCollins Publishers.

FIRST ECCO PAPERBACK EDITION PUBLISHED 2021

Designed by Michelle Crowe

Library of Congress Cataloging-in-Publication Data has been applied for.

ISBN 978-0-06-297746-5 (pbk.)

21 22 23 24 25 LSC 10 9 8 7 6 5 4 3 2 1

for my parents

+

for my sisters

The non-autonomous machines . . .
multiplied power through external operation
by human or animal muscle or by natural forces.

Autonomous machines
were internalized models of the ordered motions
of the celestial spheres.

The first were symbols of power.
The second, of order.
Both were fundamental to the new value system.

—CAROLYN MERCHANT, *The Death of Nature*

CONTENTS

✛

✛

+

+

+

+

I LOOKED ON MY RIGHT HAND AND BEHELD

a hand made out of all that it touched—
fingers of syringes packed with soiled
polyester blankets nails cut from

a plastic bottle cap knuckles
shaped by rinds of other knuckles
and details layered in delicate ash—

ruddy, colorful, clothed. But the left,
flesh and gray, poured like the concrete
surrounding it and sanded at the edges

careful as geometry allows with
dried skin creeping through contours.
Naked hands. Beating knuckles on the ground

wondering will it crack the concrete finally
will it crumble under opposing forces—
material, economy as simple as concrete

is simple, simple to explain but difficult
to understand without explanation.
As plates in our deep crust skid past

one another. One might wonder who
thinks to pour a building of mostly
liquid. Such is the logic of conviction

we are told before the terms are defined.
Dysfunction of episodic memory.
Episode of memory of dysfunction.

Hands that are not our hands.
And so convinced are we of
our own demise we devise it.

THE LOTUS ON MARINA BAY SPEAKS

I am master of the evening lightshow.
Come 8 o'clock, sun gone,
The people belong to me & my
    electric arsenal.

They quit their shiny surfaces & sharp objects.
Take off their pointing typing fingers,
abandon their minute-made stances
    until tomorrow.

For now it is time to watch lightforms dance
color across glass & marinawater.
Watch them gather, nod to greet each other,
    newly deferent.

Here the black-iris bulb blinks from a lightboat,
sashays into a beam of seagreen, soon to be engulfed
by that sandstorm of lightflecks—henna-orange &
    desert-clay red.

Sometimes I pretend they understand
my show. That my captivating demonstration
might demonstrate something. To them.
    Inside them.

But that is not the case. Not my place. After all
they stuffed the ARTSCIENCEMUSEUM into
my pistil. My petalfingers are padded with
    glass skylights.

Yesterday I heard the small man in black
hissing into his handheld device. He wants
to make a deal. Wants to sell the Marina Bay
        Sands Hotel.

If the deal goes through they will appoint
a CREATIVEDIRECTOR. What does this deal
mean for me. The towers gleam
        behind me.

I am master of the evening lightshow.
Come 8 o'clock, sun gone,
the people belonged to me & my
        electric arsenal.

OBJECT AT THE DEPARTMENT STORE SPEAKS

Listen, take me with you. You have so many things to look at.
    I want you to see where your black gashes for eyes reach
    for depth. I have these ruby eyes. I can see edges.
    Edges are shadowy, maybe have rings. I know the meaning

of an instant because I saw someone die in one—
    I was debrided from contused flesh. I see the planet in your belly.
    It is dense with instants. The planet in my belly is painted green.
    I do not much like this mezzanine. My fourteen-karat

peers are formless. Spineless too. Look at them slump
    there. They have gems for eyes but cannot make meaning
    as I do. The architecture of the eye is complex—
    I can draw diagrams and walk you by lighted buildings

to help you understand your black gashes better.
    So take me home. Do it. Slip me into your pinkish hand
    in the dressing room, buy kohl from the ground floor
    to thwart suspicion. Walk out with your clavicles pointed

at the guards behind you like flesh encrusted handguns.
    No matter that you stole me from a department store.
    We are all stolen. What is possessing. Who was
    our clientele during the last great recession.

THE TAMPING IRON SPEAKS

> . . . *the powder exploded, carrying an iron instrument*
> *through his head an inch and a fourth in circumference, and*
> *three feet and eight inches in length* . . .
> —*The Boston Post*, SEPTEMBER 21, 1848

Here is business enough for you.
Business is a practice, it is.
Of railroad tracks and the train.
Of boxcar slats. Of that which
is always approaching—

can you see my explosion?
Can you see my ungentle
approach? From the blacksmith's
smithy I pack and tamp to blast
black powder into the blast hole

and become myself. Unlike a person.
I know what a person is. I was once
damp with one. See my glia stain,
my inscription. For a short moment
I had an eye on this flat face. I could

believe. Now I am flat. Am a face.
Cannot break this glass case, cannot

set blast—light fuse—
will angle—at which I enter
bedrock.

THE LEVEE SPEAKS

With my hands but it was with the wire

    The way a train on a cantilever truss bridge switches tracks for distance
    from the freeway but the switch rails are loose and it hurtles
    into the river below

The wire was white but the wire was red

    Or a drawbridge lifting to let a barge pass beneath
    to find the barge is too large
    and knew it

With my car I drove her from the Winn-Dixie from
Winn-Dixie to the levee under the bridge

    of a time he was in his car
    looking for her

    The way an aisle at the Winn-Dixie
    the aisle at the Winn-Dixie never ends

Red yes red

    Or skin slowly scraped away to reveal an innermost exhaustion
    which would rather walk skinless
    than not at all

With the red wire and the filaments braided clockwise inside

    The way the war doctor would rather amputate the arm
    than ligate the artery

The wire but the wire

    a phased yaw mark of a massive
    contraption the caprice and fullness of whose movement and body
    recedes unperceived

    Encyclopædia Britannica and its list of great inventions
    (profound effects on human life) lists
    the polygraph

With wind's change in course a traffic cone tips off the bridge follows the river
miles downstream miles from intention

    The way wire sways from a telephone pole
    by the levee after a storm
    not wanting
    to hurt anyone with the wind

The wire I wrapped it twice

    twisted counterclockwise
    into fiber inside it

SILENT AUCTION

Yes I helped decree it.
In the white-walled
room of before with
strangers + veils.
Don't think I don't think
about it daily. Up here
fumigating my oriel
according to the Newer
Ordering. I feel exactly
how we got here. We
thought. Then we did
as we thought. Then
answered + when we
answered how we did
as we thought
what was was
no one could afford
the self-inducing
covenant. You'd be
surprised what little
we, the slighter figures
there among the rest,
could do in the room,
strobing like sightlines
in the jetbridge.
Now we'll never see
the men who appraise us
through the one-way
mirrors. Forevermore is

bidding. Every time
I enter the hall, leaving
my liquid assets pooling
in the center of my
oriel, I feel less prepared
for the day—+ no
I won't know it's coming—
when they quit me here
entirely + pooling
in the trespasses of my
last remaining asset.

THE CRYPTOGRAPHER SPEAKS

And there is no panic.
It doesn't fit in. The cracks
of the sidewalk are filled when
concrete is poured. Fill
them with nail clippings.
Extra product. That
is how excessive we can be.
And resourceful, masters
of manufacture. Now do you know
what dust is? The chime
that signals entry into
the convenience store.
It shadows knowledge
of the system. It is testimony.
Anyone can rub it out
with his sleeve. Knowing
or unknowing. The vaultish
powder is a diagram. It is
a torquetum. It is divined
for patent secrets. I can hear
you speak when I twist my key—
your destination must
precede your map.

ON ATRAZINE

I.

"Well I drank it," says the scientist
when they ask him what he has
done with the contaminated
water. "There is less in the lab's
cesspool than you have us
suck in past our teeth."

II.

Underneath the dying broadleaf
between rows of cornstalks
an African dwarf frog
twists his drying-out tongue
shakes a webbed foot
in the direction of his pond
behind the cornfield—
cannot move, that
amphibian ambivalence
mocked by the oocytes
now in his testes, splitting
into ovum. José María
bends down, tender hand
passing cracked boot to scoop
the thirsty vertebrate onto
the cushion of his palm.
Walks as if on a tightrope
through the stalks to the pond
to deliver him.

III.

Point-oh-one parts per
billion castrates the frog
twenty-four thousand
parts per billion
and José María will sleep
in the field—

STYLIZED FACTS

Now I can't
get past the mezzanine,
never know who's waiting
for me downstairs
by the revolving door
covered in shields or crosses
like the blood drive. Will this
be the year they finally succeed
in harvesting these last
self-organs, I ask, as they
tell me it's for a cause?
As if I'm not the swollen one
smiling on their pamphlets.
Don't bother with this logic
of sameness as you eye me
like the platter at Labor Lunch.
I used to envy the trees
wearing mists as veils,
modest trunks exploding into
thousands of muscle-bound
legs soon as they reach
the soil. Now even trees
seem docile and susceptible.
So too for the quasi-
goddesses with half-lives
shorter than a hair's.
When we still had hair
and partners my partner
shaving said hair said

we should be made of light.
While every morning I
wake hoping to uncover
some slab of my body
hollowed out and encased
in steel. Everyone's entitled
to her own magic bullet
theory of self. There's
the get-to-know-you
game we play no longer
for we lost *get-to* and *know-you.*
If you had to press further into
the future in what county what
province would you elect
what version of what self?

A half-frozen field late
January. Tall, spare, lone
turbine thrashing by
the abandoned interstate.

I play my game.

I await the next campaign.

HOW WE PROGRAMMED THE APOCALYPSE

Remember the sonic attack? Kind of like that.

Simulate the sounds of crickets, then decimate the crickets.

Sounds of a lover who can see in sixteen colors.

Sound of un-dread heretofore heard only by the dead.

Soon the people hear our sound. Each wants her own

private symphony. In a long queue they gradually accrue.

From a distance they seem to stretch continuous,

smoothly defined as a smile line. But up close?

One sees discontinuities. Up-raised fists, cupping palms.

Trading sundries. Shouldering past sisters and Sundays.

Casting around for ways to afford the sound.

Neighbor came to mean She Who Queued in My Vicinity.

As the queue shortened everyone could afford it.

Then everyone was plural: *data*. Everything

served and being served on metal servers.

It was never our intent to punctuate the sentences

of others. But now it's late. Too late to unstate our

importance. And besides, the crickets died for this.

Pulses quicken, slipping across our screens.

We play the quieting machines. We pity the soon unseen.

A thought arrives. Ask forgiveness instead?

No. Everyone we pity dies. The rest rust in line.

SILENT AUCTION

Look what we did to me   inside the sun

warm blue hue   my varnish cracking

ice sheets   gliding

nothing clings to me   see the trail of hair

wisping behind me   we have done this

I measure constant flux   + it is not a transit

I meter constant albedo   + it is not eclipse

nothing left when   we measure the amplitudes

what is left when   we circumscribe a wave

do I salt the sea   + curl myself into it

or salt the sea   with stinging ants

if only I might bathe again   (when)

if only I might eat again   (when)

what I mean when   (when) I say matter is

I will give this to you   but you will give it back

HUTTONIAN THEORY OF EARTH

When the swallows haul up into sky
we would correct their color with digital
projection. We would look into the eye
of the projector. It will singe our retinas.
Make lace of them. We swoon
over the geometry of vision. It is
the geometry of a postcard plus a point.

Sleeping above rooftops I hear a truck
loading / unloading as the dawn still
takes requests. Its long low lowing
the desperate voice of granite pushing
metamorphic schist or the corporate
announcement that another uncomformity
has been amassed by the seabed.

But you know this. You finger the palmlines
of the seafloor. Tell me does evolution fail

to track independent truth or must we construct
finer tools, weightier estimations? Tell me—

ON STYROFOAM

Despite the fruitfly's humming gusto often

I believe my waste hazardous, the jaundiced

innards of an apple now laced with human blight—

hazard produced as I consume I cannot escape

the thought. I peel the sticking stigma off

the table to immure it in the Styrofoam cup

with traces still of rooibos. I hazard how

Styrofoam is borax and heat, expansion

blithe as a solid can be and

the thermal resistance of the hoof

of an ox. How thoroughly opposed

to flesh. Fathom the body in the Bar

where Ray Krone throws darts. Or Ray McIntire

when he makes a life raft for

the U.S. Coast Guard (Styrofoam is

after all ninety-nine percent air

enough to save a life). And

the first inklings of napalm in an adjacent

cell cavorting with plutonium triggers—

the Inventors Hall of Fame

inducts McIntire just four years

after Arizona inducts Krone into freedom

again, and as I write

Styrofoam insulation products

save billions in energy costs.

I too am only the expansion

of polymers when, as the apple

was once exuberant and whole,

I remember the time in the park

after the afternoon bell I charged

my teeth into my forearm and the force

hurtled me over myself and I knew new

power as trace as mark and said

mom look what sister did to me

TRIPLE WITCHING

That's not smog sitting on the lake
but smoke blown south from the fires
in Saskatchewan. The sky never asks
our opinion and yet we charge all manner
of missive through it, casual as the first
man (surely it was "man") who cried
"This is mine" or the man who believed him.
I do not know whose smoke-curtain
this is, falling now to subdue,
pressing down over humming
flesh and interaction.

But I think my chest is a pocket of sky—
slow, heart. Speed, up and up.
Find. Cadence, frequency at which to
resist, enclosure. Oppose motion.
Suspend of ever-maddening.
Frenzy, maddening for want of
space, volatility implied by the threat of
expiration. The nothing-and-every-
thing-to-lose. As we turn down to sleep
the nocturnal crowds in bushes and
trees play from where we have paused.
A gnat traps himself in my left ear.
Options—drone, hum, buzz—expire.

WAR OF THE CURRENTS

Telephone lines gallop outside.
    They trace lines in palms. Surmise
these poles are our trees now. Palm after palm.
    I'm lucky my

currents alternate, can be direct,
    conform to National Electrical Safety
Code, conform the way George Fore-
    man's indoor/outdoor grill cools

on a countertop even as the power grid
    ails. The grid is not cerebral.
In its circuitry is systematic. Does not
    employ given-to-us structures. Deploys

those agreed-upon—lattice not
    scale-free, lattice not small-
world, lattice not Erdös-Rényi-random—
    & remember the blackout, remember

the solar flare, remember forgetting the complex
    conduits, vast, unseen, busy with volts,
fragile. I can take single or split phase
    supply streams. I can take the pastoral nodes

& urban junctions & make them less dependable.
    A spatial network. Dependence
lends trouble to the interdependent.
    If only knotgrass might act

with quick & unanticipated collapse, lapse
    fragile as our overwhelmed, unwell trelliswork,
courses invisible. Split phase. Single phase.
    Phase LOCK. Phase shift.

We are all in, all in to achieve our
    economies of scale which achieve
the opposite of balance, traffic flows toward defeat—
    what is economy but this train on which

a conductor wakes sleepers before the last stop,
    cues the soprano, mutes the horn
without pausing to sense we all conduct well, well
    enough that it is tough to engineer

a quick & anticipated death, death
    by fibrillation by two thousand volts—
prophase, metaphase, anaphase: continues.
    Phase LOCK. Phase out—

Last month a utility pole made news in Mariposa County.
    Was charged with manslaughter after
lighting a wildfire. They called it
    negligence. Call it revolt. Call it warning.

GENERALIZED METHOD OF MOMENTS

Find moments like tiny razors.
Arrange into blades. Harvest them
as a leisure gardener. First yield, gloved
and methodical. Impose structure.
Inspect roots. Inspect stems for infection.
Or pluck them unhandily. Wings
off a fruitfly before the dreaded experiment.

But too often   the moments   find you.
Arrive   in legislated chaos   hurtled
By a   chagrined wind,   sandstorm
of needles—   eddy of nettle-hairs . . .
How   to order in   the midst
the mist   of the stinging field,
where memory is   a rash in the tall

grass. Moments as hives. As slices
of indifference from which to estimate
some parameter of interest.
Blinking, eyelids too become blades.
The scrim of our error matrix
shudders with imprecision.
It shakes itself out. We forget.

⏻ TRIAL FOR THE NEW AUBADE

Day is brushing the brush off my back. No. Dawn is
tracing the margin of my being with unpleasant certainty.
Today is a truck? It shakes this structure in which we sleep.
Yes. That's our new definition of dawn. No reason to share
dawns these days with strangers. And that something so arbitrary
as *Sun* played scheduler for so many centuries?—like *Feudalism*,
then *Welfare State*. Like secrets swelling in your absence.
In my new dawn you are barely a face. Inkblot eyes and mouth
a simple laceration. You know how easily you appear
in the corner of my vision to remind me where I am not,
in the corner of what I am not to remind myself of,
in the corner of my screen to furl, unfurl, *tap*, there, there's
the slender magnet arresting the iron flecks of my data . . .
You will betray me. Leave me alone unsure of my own
periphery. My eyes, these tiny factories of forgiveness,
at what rate will my optic machinery depreciate—do I worry
about these decreasing returns to scale? The splat sound
of the shower water as I wring my hair in my new dawn. My day,
my data, how much of you do I lose with this dawn?

1ST TRIAL FOR THE NEW AUBADE

Does the season match the birdsong,
did I hear the birdsong over the white noise machine,
who brought the white noise machine here,
was it the other, heaving next to me under a shroud,
for how many seasons has he/she been sleeping here
next to me, was there a logic of want to begin with
in a seaside town or a dark box rattling underground,
did he/she come through a revolving door like the termite
winding up through the drain of my sink basin,
was there a seasonal contract or perpetual exchange,
who installed this sour drain in my middle, is it time
to adjust my angles, for whom, whom today, tomorrow,
what is history cloaking, as burlap wraps around wet figs,
is there a logic of want, when will my season match my song.

2ND TRIAL FOR THE NEW AUBADE

There are hands on my body, how many.
Do they belong to the other, heaving.
These hands that want to touch me, my skin.
A burlap wrap around the roots. A transplanted tree.
I just remembered how these hands came in here.
Was it the last blond moon after the last
full day. I strayed beyond my sliding door
to switch off the terrace lamp. A figure spilled out
of shadow. As if night had waited all those
years. Time is indexed by tones of abandon.
Whose. On the terrace the logic of want
placed one by one its hands on my body.
It invited itself. Now day after day
my body tenses. The hands never flinch.

FRAGMENTS FROM THE IMAGINED EPIC:
THE SONG OF HAVE BLUE

the hawk moth alone detects Lockheed's
Nighthawk **%** Nighthawk's faceted wings **%**
the energy that might announce his design
% Nighthawk is stealthy **%**

sister was afraid of darkness
% put her in boots and hat **%** rustled
in the leaves **%** "See better, night friend" **%**
"we too can steal, have inward-canted stabilizers

to countermeasure us manned demonstrators"
% on the waistline of a woman on sand in slack
desert night the hawk moth listens, shifts pin-
feet on her skin **%** skin stretched taut across pelvic

bones **%** translucent under the moon's glow
% desert sways beneath the survivable
testbed **%** the woman lusts **%** sketches circles
in the sand with the bone that bisects the crest

of her pelvis **%** for Nighthawk **%** for Nighthawk
snuck into this night his up-swept wing to sigh **%**
sister has joined to fight him with him **%**
a more honest blue hue to say have blue

% say that her pelvis too is faceted
as his wings % sister sighs %
lusts for Nighthawk's stolen maiden flight %
pelvis dips into sand % "you are more beautiful,"

whispers the hawk moth to Nighthawk %
"than anything I've let myself sing to"

THE WAR GONE WRONG ROOM

More like the maximum-security playground on the street with all the riots.
More hedgefund-glass enclosures as if the riots were landscape,
with waterfall. More cross armed supervisors with first-aid kits
strapped onto ankles, next to pistols. More puzzling over numbers
like *truth* : how many watering cans . . . and *truth* : how long 'til the color
left her . . . and *dare* : take the scent of metal off take Alice's hands off
the monkey bars . . . More like playgroundless—more tangling in nets
more ropes for nets to avoid the void below. More no-ground ground.
More forts, more bows, more sterns. More ornately decorated wheels
in the helm, please. More play to distract from lack of ground. More so
now that Alice is no more. Moreover, what of the supervisors?
More budget cuts. More for your dollar? More for the Dollar. More
exotic juice in the juiceboxes to trade with the bullies. More juice
to burn into smoke to soot up the ceiling fan. More keypads to catch
our twiddling thumbs. More tangling bodies in nets. More nets
filling with corpses. More decals for ships and chests. More juice
to bargain for, then burn. More fire blankets on our lungs. More
casual more indifference. Mere casualties. More Alice can you hear her?
More distant grows Alice. "More?" she moans, "it just keeps going."
More war gone wrong. More wounds. More soon. More keep going
don't stop no. More please no. More I can't. More can't breathe.

OBJECTIVITY AS BLANKET

Nor the police, hyenas on hearing five confessions, four false and
one too irresistible. Nor the mental health elephant, tusked by the state.
Nor the common sense stork twisting at the prosecutor's feet. Nor the one
the one juror, uneasy facing eleven pale sheep that bay all day
all night for conviction. Nor the Governor, sir! Nor the common sense
stork, now in a knot. Nor the shots. Nor the clause, unbending. Nor
the clause, bending. Nor, seeing his fitful approach, did one turn back
to flip the window latch for the lifeform nearly breaking himself on glass.
Nor the next Governor. Nor the state—carriage horses trotting ever
steady blinders acute to the eye. Nor the widower how could he, puma
in pull-focus. Nor the defense counsel, not for lack of it. Nor the stork,
is she breathing? Is there such a thing as breathing here and does it mean—?
The polyester the royal blue the blanket on the bed of the mother of two.

SILENT AUCTION

Please let me tell you what it is to make market. Paint the sky Purple-K. Hospital gown-blue. Parent's house violet. Daub above the fiscal river I can see from my office oriel. Where I am writing now. Pretty pricing patterns contain damning dispatches. Think of the market as your rain. It is rain. High frequency rain and there is never a highest bidder. It is bullets. Blown to sky and deflected. High frequency bullets filling the sea with their shells. Pick this one. Pick high frequency. Pick no one.

You are in bed with your stun gun. We have a market failure. We prepare to cover the sky. In sodium bicarbonate. We already have empire. Let us make market. Here. Where. The other side is shadows. The huddling audience bids against us. Against time. Against blueprint. The negative space is time. It is not enough to press into vellum and displace natural dye. Vellum that came from ancient mammoth? The mammoth ate stellar gas. At noon time. Being too large noon for him is always. Be too large. Amortize the sun.

PAWN SLIP

How hard to price a loan. How simple to tell a story—
eke out a life in sentences. Themes, motifs, old mares
in dreams—but a day here is like a day no where. How
heat here rises, is also white. Hundred thirty degrees
up there, hundred seventy-five, hundred ninety-two.
Wardens worry about diabetes type II, hepatitis,
innocence, all factors which increase incidence of
heat-related illness. What is earthed in the prison limits?

Four million pounds of vegetables. Generous lodgings
for a few thousand brood cows whose young have
futures more explicitly traded. A match for the signature
on a pawn slip. A travel clock a silver ring a pocket
watch. Possession is a pledge and a pledge is proof
of what might have been but probably wasn't.
Which is the wind that nuzzles the wall and enters
the chamber. A jeweler is an investor long on metals.

Possession is also a position. Carbon paper prostrate
against a paper slip. A travel clock a silver ring a pocket
watch. Possession is a pledge and a pledge is proof
of what might have been but probably wasn't.
Which is a story. Stories do not heed the danger
in counterfactuals nor recognize their brokering value.
The state's compensation sums to eleven thousand per year,
but if he didn't prove the value of the collateral
                                        they'd destroy it.

THE LIST

at the Heart Institute

Who lords this list anyway. Whose lists is
the lord of this list on. Eighty days of next
on the list after a lifetime of lists. Of

strip-mined tar sands + petrified dunes.
Creasing the terrain of your forehead.
Behind which blinking synapses wait.

Restless geothermal features. The city also
waits. Heaving + short of breath, strapped in
by busy blood-bridges. Red taillights mirror blue

headlights. Color-coded weight cresting toward
some walled-off core. Machine that gives
+ receives. The city (your body) is full of division.

Welcomes metal + flesh. Vestigial appendages.
Futuristic ordnance. The hungry + fed mingle
in aortic alleys. The well + unwell mosh in your

rib cage. Rib cage as runaway truck ramp. As layby.
New home to active-duty batteries extracted from
the broken flashlight. Carrier for ammo + gun

from the just-dead soldier. Rewired
stand-in for the melting circuit on the fuse box.
Snug cavern for the exiled apostle—

would we take to it as we took to your son
would you take to it as you took to your wife
would it take after you like your son takes

your hand now, fingers contorted around
your thumb like veins dodging behind
the vena cava, as the nurse announces the news.

Pulsing from a heap of crackling synapses
the small bivalve machine you are waiting for
unpledges its allegiance to another body veering

off the curve of homeostatic indifference. The body
skids into a plane of infinitesimal mirrors. This still-
splintering stranger is our gift no more lists—

we will take to it as we took to your son
you will take to it as you took to your wife
will it take after you like the other father

whose son is not tugging the gauze of your wife's
moss-green dress as she lifts him onto your hospital bed.
The other father whose son's body the slow moss

arranges to cover. Body in surrender. To surrender
is to empty oneself of allegiance. So that all sums
are zero-sum. So that the moss may take its place.

PROXY MEANS

a test. In a morning
blue suit the Census Taker
drops his credentials
and picks them up

by a lanyard
gingered in the red dust
between his shiny black
shoes.

The eyes in the village
hide. The glinting wink
of the sun is in
the Census Taker's shoes.

The laminated Census
Taker marches to procure
evidence. Evidence of
need. Evidence of

mistake. This Census
Taker tells them
what they have.
What they need

to mean and promises
protection. Proxy means
need. The Census Taker
enumerates proxies for

means. What stove,
what kind of stove.
How much kerosene.
Take your identification

card. Take care.
Do they really make TVs
so big. How much kerosene
per month. How many deaths

occurred in your empty
cupboard. Don't look
at the shoe. Who
after all is living.

Here.

DIVISION DAY

I.

Perhaps a detailed appendix will do.
On the measurement of birthweight
in this environment. Triangulate
the measure across facility records. What
is *record*, I ask you. Neonatal
weight loss is known to be quite severe.
Who did not lose 10% (of something)
within 24–48 hours of being born? Is
there reason to trust maternal recall
in this setting. Given the centrality
of this measure please test there is no
clustering—around round numbers—
that the number of deaths accords roughly
with regional averages—that the data
satisfy Benford's Law, that they could
not have been invented in the bedlam
of birth, of being born. And to record?
Why the forensic attitude is a question
I've learned to no longer ask. Here, a
new year, we are on a rural health mission.

We have helical insignia on our lapels.
We have a census; we have maps, we have
museum. These institutions code what we
owe only incompletely. There may be pockets
of space that destroy the information falling
into them. Those would form evidence
of a similar kind. Evidence of a similar
paradox, a paradox of information.

II.

I am trigger happy as the horizon
of a black hole. Today I am a fantastically small
coefficient. Yesterday I was helical as hellfire.
Always I feel at home in acid rain, it burrows
into pores to locate the core of me, impurity
joining the spine with all its familial plasmic
fluids. One rainy day, you will find me
naked but for the black shroud of my own
ambition, folded in a geometry you have
seen before. As that night, remember when?
Coming home I couldn't in my compromise
stand up to gravity stepping out of the taxi,
fell, held onto the grate of the sewage drain
like a handle to wring out my neck and
look up at you. *This is how I will remember
you* you said and you did not mean to say
something hurtful. We are full of saying,
coding rhymes, one dog-tag dropping
into a bin of them, after the division
enters the system, entered by whom, by

UNIQ_ARMY_ID // DOB // HOME-

TOWN // YRS_SERVED // by near-tragic

longing for uncompromised completeness.

When you find me in that naked geometry

of compromise I will tell you I never lied

to you, I will tell you I cannot to you or

in general lie, tell you I cannot even if

I wanted to lie about all that I have forgotten.

III.

Division is a form of forgetting.
You know Photograph 51 that breathy
out-of-focus evidence, discovery
of the geometry of information.
See the scatter diffracted the strands
antiparallel the curvature the crucial
crystallographic patterns of restriction
restricting parameters—our iron-clad
cardinality is bound up in this hellfire
of helices. As I struggle to zip my skirt
arms contorted, zipper behind me,
light patterns inching across my wall,
I am Rosalind Franklin who in
the same motion discovered a bulge, her
skirt would not zip, friends asked if she
could be pregnant. In a way she was—
raped by x-rays, pregnant and bulging
with division. Uterus absorbing
the shock of discovery not as a martyr
but as a fantastically small coefficient.

How many times such attacks have

been leveled against me. You think your

self so self-contained. Abstemious with

respect to influence. As if to record

is to be neutral. When my colleague asks

how are you doing today what I want to say is

what Franklin was known to say often:

I am good, though female.

IV.

Division occurs when we exit with or
without intention one ruthless enclosure
for another. As when I exit your kitchen
every Sunday after you have painted
for several hours a portrait of me reading
the same page over and over I leave my best
blouse on the coatrack between sittings—
black silk. Thick knuckle-sized knots
for buttons. *Is it too warm in here*, what tone.
Your stacks of inverted-color photographs
of travels, of ephemera, photographs taken
by one camera through the viewfinder
of another. *That's Prussian blue below your
lower lip.* If a machine were to photo-shoot
division day it would also have two lenses
in inexact relation to one another. I have
learned to thrive on these inexact relations
stemming from my own vexed dualism,
from my understanding that the number
attached to me at birth was all too trust-

worthy, from my acknowledgment that

division occurs on day one for too many,

from my desire to be washed on that day

divine day of divisive resolution in acid

rain, misguided forensics, UNIQ_ID //

DOB // HOMETOWN, I am

a fantastically small coefficient but not

yet small enough, let me be *self* let me

be finally fantastically alone.

V.

As when the father opens the door

for the prophet drinks the wine at the empty

seat and closes the door again.

The eyes of the family open again.

Measurement, outcome,

we have museum. You there. You

are fidgeting in your seat, burn most

of your daily caloric intake this way,

shuffling your proud joints past

each other. I know, you would dive

out of your own lithe already-godlike

body to be that prophet, harbinger

of never-forgetting, for being him

you might justify your bearish but

inevitable bearing on geometry,

on the hellish helix of history—

shift, slide, rise, tilt, roll, twist—

on the field equations that describe

a tender invitation, the elegant

curve of the neck of a black hole.

You remember all the details so that
you will not become one—shear,
stretch, buckle, stagger, pitch, tip,
propeller—when will you give up
this self-image, self-as-singular, self-
as-self, same, separate, singularity?

VI.

I woke alone in a hotel, where?

Perhaps where *finally* is meaningless.

Why was I not afraid. I am always

afraid with you. Yesterday I was told

black holes are not as black. Not as I am

afraid. With you the sun is fragile

as the constant. Speed of light.

Yesterday I was told information

can escape, can hold shape on exit,

the sun also a shape inside eyelids.

The morning in the hotel, woke.

To evidence. Pewter chargers

on linen, smoked fish. Morning

in the hotel. Woke to poached eggs—

pewter chargers smoked fish wedge

of lemon—there was someone else

here. Imagine the coefficient. Still,

life. Bring me a scale. There was

someone else here. Still let me be

coefficient. Fantastically small.

There is someone else here.

FRAGMENTS FROM THE IMAGINED EPIC:
THE ISLAND OF STONE MONEY

ONE

*I exchanged a small short-handled axe for a good white rai,
fifty centimeters in diameter.*

I
need an
axe

or
something
to axe

my
weeds I
need

TWO

For another rai, a little larger, I gave a fifty-pound bag of rice.

a house. Whose
house. That house.
The one with copra
and rice inside.

One to grow out
of. Step out. To hoist
on my shoulders and
throw at the men

in pants. What do
we have that they need.
We have stone. We have
strong straight backs.

THREE

*I was told that a well-finished rai, about four feet
in diameter, is the price usually paid either to
the parents or to the headman of the village as a
compensation of the theft of a mispil [woman].*

In pants is all he is today. And yesterday. And envious.
He is envious of the net of interlocking hands that leaves us alone.
We can be left alone. The net an inverted parachute conveys and bears our
unswerving value. He is jealous of our system of value. He and his kamerads
are colorless prisms protruding from the earth, ruts in earth eczemic as the
Spanish suzerains before them.   As the Spanish before them
they strip-mine the fissures   of our seashells. Take
     the shells too. Call them   aragonite. I am one
     of many stones that says   *Bezirksamt.* You are
          the one with the vocabulary to say these things. I am the anti-
               pneumatic. The numismatic. Who's to say numeraire.
                    A stone lost at sea is strong as a
                    villanelle sung in stone.

A five days voyage. Longer in storm.

Come bearing betel nut. Come bearing form.

For the man at the mine site. Bring your seashell adze.

Feel the flintstrike of value when you cleave the cold-clad stone.

Take coral, a large piece grind   circles in stone-center.

What makes this difficult. The   tools are softer than

stone. Hence labor. Why the hole.   For transport. For all

future loans. Where is the bamboo raft? As sturdy as the last? So many lost at

sea. We are like joules. If I were you I'd begin. To conduct business in joules. I

am one of many stones with a black X in paint. I am the one leaning.

Into the bosom of a house. My owner will earn me back.

He is smoothing the roads. No, we enjoyed it.

The way our roads teased our feet.

The feathers of the blos-bird

sweeping faces in the gale.

A five days voyage. Longer in storm.

Come bearing betel nut. Come bearing form.

For the man at the mine site. Bring your seashell adze.

The flintstrike of value when you cleave the cold-clad stone.

Take coral, a large. Piece grind circles in center.

Make this difficult. The tools are softer than.

Labor. Why the hole. For transport. For all future.

Is the bamboo raft as. Sturdy as the last. So lost at sea.

We are like joules. Do you conduct business in joules. I do.

As I am one of many. Stone with a black **X** in paint.

I am the one leaning to the bosom of a house.

My owner will earn me back as.

The roads teased our feet.

FOUR

I am the stone lost at sea, there is a hole
at my center. / A stone lodged in the fold
of the sea. / I am still dense with value. Why am
I missing a center. / What is arrogant. Simply know I
am. Am smoother and bigger. / The Blarney Stone. Someone is
proud to call me *his*. / I am the stone. Lost at sea. There is a hole. At my
center. / It takes a special. Power to remain here.
And belong to a different. Man every so often. To
change hands. / I am still dense with value. Why
am I missing the center. / The hands hold me as. The grains
of sand that outline the stone / of Gibraltar. Only the sea is *my* owning!
Mine. I am. / I am the stone lost at sea. The hole is my center. / Without
me the richest man would not be rich. Several / Others would be evicted.
That is how money works. / I am still dense with value. Right where
I'm missing a center. / So say I cannot reproduce / But am worth
more in baskets than was quarried for. / Am the stone. Lost at
sea. There is a hole. / My center. I am still, I am the missing.

DIFFERENCE ENGINE

Born, never asked.
As biofilm huddles
in a freshwater fissure
of the dead sea floor.

Born, never asked.
Like the swollen
recruit at the bottom
of the pyramid.

Born, never asked.
Tasked uniformless
in a torn-open trench
with a machine gun.

Born, never asked.
Into this jetbridge
full of people who.
Who are they.

Born, never asked
to enter the engine.
Engine's bronze gears
and double-high teeth.

Born, never asked.
Now shivering
down the fire
escape in a column . . .

Enter a window
to a dark room
full of a person.
Add. Exit to shiver

down another
floor. One of us
per column per
floor. The us floor

then leave. On one
floor my difference
is a woman. I add
her. Have I

added no one.
Before this floor.
Make the room
warm enough to feel

my mouth. It stings.
I'm not preparing
to leave. Don't count-
down. Leave me or

(fissure pyramid jet-
bridge trench eng-
ine) could the funct-
ion be.

PERNKOPF *ATLAS* (I)

Volume Two. Thorax, Abdomen and Extremities,
with 378 Illustrations, Most in Color.
Apt that Fig. 1 presents external form of a female
breast and chest, surface, grayscale,

intact and mapped region by region
with a fan of bayonets sketched to this or that
latinate term. Each term a whisper, a small assertion
taken as consent, collateral. As ransom.

> *Preparatory work done to gain access to deeper*
> *regions (e.g. the cutting of muscles, reflection of parts,*
> *disarticulations and separation of muscles and blood*
> *vessels by means of retractors) has not been explained*
> *in the legends when the steps in the preparation were*
> *self-evident.*

The human figure is self-evident, I have often thought—
its only evidence is itself. We draw definitions to learn,
draw nude models in studio classrooms to learn
about shadow, draw the dead to discover what casts it

and why definition does not always suffice.
Draw with Fig. 88, the hand, collateral. An extremity's
extremity. Fingers, more extreme. Ring
and pinky ones untouched touching the page.

The cut begins at top-center of the middle finger
fingernail down the now-blue tendon
to the watchline. Another cut, perhaps along it.
There is a crease on my wrist where my hairband sits

when I sleep with my hair down. There is always hair
where extremity begins. On pulled-away skin, the flap,
a tattoo which even in death this hand cannot escape,
a signature heavy with, without. Signature

is an invention of death, in fact, like words
themselves. *Anatomie des menschen* or *untermenschen?*—
semantics too are life or deadly. And legacy. In Fig. 321:
legacy parallels legs the way a willow in a Viennese garden

affirms and denies the city with its branches. What branch
am I and where do the veins in my left and right hands
coalesce on their long journey back to the heart?
Exquisite drawings make answers too precise.

Did the anatomists ever climb out of themselves
to watch from above, from dorsal then ventral view,
ever survey their desks with watercolors, cadavers,
surrounding brushes, pencils, palettes also

scalpels, forceps, occasionally drawn into view?
This intersection of craft and thought, body at
the center, accretes meaning with every
blot, every nib, I begin
                    to smell
                    the flesh
                    as it gets
                    torn away,
                    layers—
                    lips and
                    labia—
                    wettest
                    in life
                    sourest
                    in death

                    but not
                    to be mis-
                    taken for
                    protest
as my own many-times-great grandfather, grandson of a
Useful Jew applied current to the brain, to cortices
of Prussian soldiers with already-fractured skulls.
And the first Jew to win a Nobel Prize?

He discovered barbituric acid, from which all barbiturates
are still made—no coincidence, as Nobel invented
dynamite, *the merchant of death is dead*
his premature obituary read before he invented
                    the prize:
                    for the advancement
                    of; for me and
                    for; for four
                    dismissed; for
                    sciens, scientis;
                    for the opposite
                    of ephemera;
                    for the lusty;
                    for illustrators;
                    for the
                    illustrated;
                    for the illustrious;
                    for the luster
                    on the back of a man
                    waiting to enter
                    the gas chamber.
                    The lights
are also hot on the withers of a filly
on a conveyor belt in the modern abattoir.
She might shiver. He will not. Turn a page
and you will wonder what scalding bronze poured

down your trachea might feel like. I feel it now.
I let it harden and if you tear my flesh away you will
do me a favor because Harvard Medical School now boasts
a four-to-one student-to-cadaver ratio and there is a waitlist

to donate, while Burke and Hare's death masks
wink to each other over clemency in a museum
overseas. Turn a page and you might hear—crunch—
the sound of a stack of paper cut by a guillotine—

crunch—might hear 1,871 slices—crunch—into
the axial plane of a man who killed a man and after 12 years
in a cell was injected, killed. He had offered to be sliced
into millimeter-thick sheets yielding 65 gigabytes of images

which demand more than 8 MacBooks
to view. Sign me up. I too will get immortal as we build
cathedrals for relics before worship. Now we have a rose
window to replace the old, a better newer millimeter-thin

stained plastinate made from a cross-section
of a noble condemned who gave his body to Science and
the sometimes-true. The wrist slices might replace
our Eucharist, the priest must serve them as the wardens served

two requested cheeseburgers the night of to the to-be-sliced
who refused them. Who is my creator or yours? Fig. 378.
According to the Uniform Anatomical Gift Act
the skin binds a book, by the law of collateral damage.

PERNKOPF *ATLAS* (II)

Volume One. Head and Neck. Making love I wonder
were they thinking of it. Of the end as I do each time?
The red of eight years softed pale by their last three months,
by prison, now the pink of the skin between my thumb

and forefinger, almost translucent, not transparent, dumb with
effort stretched in two directions, comfortable when rounded
against this cylinder, pressed against the intimate, inanimate,
against all that stands too tall against liberty. I hear their

sighs with me and go to them. Hear the pink and read red
as the red orchestra, brilliant, uncaptured, never watercolor.
Something flowers in her. So rarely are women criminals
we know little about female parts. So rarely, in fact,

this Nazi anatomy is used to demonstrate that rape
itself is contraception. Yes someone actually believes that,
he lives a short flight from me, a flight to get on which
I wouldn't even get frisked. Remember that stern airport security

woman in Amsterdam, tight burnt orange with buttons?
Ran her hands all over concentrated two fingers on my labia,
pressed hard into them, why did she let me pass?
I think of her when I slip into kilt and roll the waistband

to make hem clear keen knees more cleanly, unstuck
to the slashes on the backs of them. How clean and tired
the world in which we learn from kin alone. Do not dissect
the frozen fetal pig, delivered from the gray warehouse.

Slice open the pregnant one digging in your yard,
flip it over and make one long clean cut along its pink-gray
underbelly, the squeals will be enveloped by history the hungry,
the shadow amoeba who emerges from your

sternum in these moments for these sounds and scents, reach
through the reddest red and fish out the fetus, relish
the warpaint staining your kilt, make holy stigmata,
laugh and lie on the lawn. Like Manet you will be loathed

for the correct placement of the heart. Cut the umbilical cord
and you can do science. *History and men enjoy a peace*
they somehow feel they earned by buying bonds or listening to a speech.
Remarkable meaning is accessible by private jet

as there is no difference between holding bonds and holding
someone in them. A bond is a promise to someday release, asking
how to find meaning in such a world misses the point entirely.
This is meaning—spontaneous, organized into new meaning

as currency wanders from cigarette to bully mark in camps
nearby and across the continent as exactly one thought
arranges itself into exactly one action across time
into crimes bigger than we ever meant to contain.

As if Sikhs would give away cured meat for free forever. As if
there were such a thing as death support. As if sex were a moral
act. Our necks sticking to hair, hair standing in for veins,
veins for arteries, are bloodless as carefully drawn legacy,

wan as encephalon drawn in an anatomy book.
Something flowers in her. I feel it too. I lust
as they lust for life and believe: *Believe with me*
in the just time that lets everything ripen.

GESTURE ATLAS

Here come the zeppelins their shapes shadow
distance. Whales that leapt and stayed— as forecast as all
becomes dirigible. Reverse thrust maneuver for mooring
and there is a floor. Stepping out on it I press in with my sock
with the equivocation of a neonate pony hair matted and
curled by placenta, by the trauma of birth stained already
as I am now with motion. With the hurry-fetch-it-now the
will-I-or-will-I-not the am-I- late-to-touch or the amorous
and the eucharist. I will not dress yet but inspect the space
between my eyes as the primary purpose of gesture
drawing is to facilitate the study of the human in motion.
Through the wall someone is watching.
Through the wall someone is watching a show.
It is anime—I think—asymptotic legs bloody but unscratched
from a fall from a tower with featureless, swift action.
I become drawn and falling. Adopt the mission
someone is saying. Search now for a missing cat. I have caves for eyes,
crevasse for nose and I forget the cat. Find a man.
A man with anamorphic memory.
He looks sideways into my caves looks for dun horses aurochs
line of dots in mineral pigment. None of us have names here.
I suspect him a clone framed into body. He suspects mine.

Slip hand into shirtsleeve. Find throwing blades. A tactical

flamethrower and this flame too is a hand. What is it

to have this world unhanded us. The alethic,

the incomputable, the lethal and lethargic?

The lethal mutation, forgetting before there is anything to

forget. The legal rotation. Angle of Proserpina's wrist upturned

with Tamar and Dinah for Rindr and Cassandra

and Leda and Philomela Medusa, Lucretia,

the Sabine women— this is the hand

that says what skin is left on my shoulder

I will abscond away from memory, that city

that could be moved to in a minute. The missing

cat. The none-of-us-have-names-here. The calisthenic how-

did-I-get-here. The joint crack of who-has-been- here. Was it

the figure in the convolution of the curtain I notice now

watching me? The figure presses the small of my back.

I falter a step and step into a cave. The hands of men

handle stacks of medallions, chips for the round. In this cave see

paintings lurid by lichens, crystals and white

mold someone has tried and failed to treat. Two caves as the time

my face folded in half and my two eyes met. Two caves meeting

are not one cave. Motionless inside this kiss *kiss me* this figure says *play.*

NOTES

I LOOKED ON MY RIGHT HAND AND BEHELD takes its title from Psalm 142:4 (KJV).

THE TAMPING IRON SPEAKS refers to the case of Phineas Gage, a railroad worker, who improbably survived injury: an iron rod shot through Gage's skull. The tamping iron is currently on display at Countway Library of Medicine.

THE LEVEE SPEAKS draws on court records from the wrongful conviction of Damon Thibodeaux, who in 1996 was charged with strangling his step-cousin to death. After eight hours of questioning, he gave a false confession. He spent fifteen years on death row in Louisiana before being exonerated by DNA testing in 2012.

ON ATRAZINE is for Tyrone Hayes, a biologist, activist, and professor at the University of California, Berkeley, who discovered that atrazine, an herbicide sprayed on most cornfields in the U.S., causes hermaphroditism in frogs. Syngenta, the company that manufactures the chemical, has attempted to discredit Hayes's research.

HUTTONIAN THEORY OF EARTH is for Felix Waechter and takes its title from mathematician and scientist John Playfair's *Illustrations of the Huttonian Theory of the Earth*. Playfair's book popularized the ideas of geologist James Hutton (1726–1797) and is widely considered to be the founding text of modern geology. Hutton's was the first scientific theory to demand a serious consideration of the concept of deep time.

ON STYROFOAM draws on details from the trial of Ray Krone, who spent ten years on death row in Arizona before his exoneration in 2002 by DNA testing. In the course of the original trial, the prosecutors asked Krone to bite into a Styrofoam cup, and claimed that the bite marks on the Styrofoam cup matched marks on the body of the victim.

TRIPLE WITCHING refers to the days on which three types of financial contracts in the U.S. securities industry expire. These days tend to see higher-than-usual trading volumes and price volatility.

GENERALIZED METHOD OF MOMENTS refers to an econometric method in which moment conditions are used to estimate parameters of statistical models.

FRAGMENTS FROM THE IMAGINED EPIC: *THE SONG OF HAVE BLUE* is named after Lockheed Martin's proof of concept (code-named Have Blue) for its first stealth aircraft, F-117 Nighthawk.

OBJECTIVITY AS BLANKET responds to the trial of Earl Washington, who spent more than seventeen years in prison in Virginia—many of them on death row—for a crime he did not commit. He was exonerated by DNA testing in 2001, through a biological sample found on a blanket at the crime scene.

PAWN SLIP responds to the conviction of Glenn Ford, who spent nearly thirty years on death row before being exonerated and released from Angola Prison in Louisiana on March 11, 2014. Ford died of complications from lung cancer on June 29, 2015.

THE LIST is for Sebastian Hitzig.

DIVISION DAY is in dialogue with Benedict Anderson's *Imagined Communities* and Stephen Hawking's final paper, co-authored with Malcolm Perry and Andrew Strominger, titled "Soft Hair on Black Holes."

FRAGMENTS FROM THE IMAGINED EPIC: *THE ISLAND OF STONE MONEY* refers to the island of Yap in the Federated States of Micronesia, where large immovable stones have been used as currency since ca. 1000 CE. Ownership of the stones is recorded through oral history and sometimes physical marks on the stones. The stones, which were quarried from distant islands, have holes in their centers to make it easier to carry them by teams of laborers. Yap was ruled by the Spanish, the Germans, and then the Japanese; when Germany bought the island in 1899, they conscripted the Yapese into labor by bankrupting the island: they took control of all the large stones in circulation by drawing black **X**s on the stones. The epigraphs are adapted from ethnographer William Henry Furness's 1910 book about the island. Economist Milton Friedman wrote a famous essay about the island, comparing the island's monetary system to the gold standard.

DIFFERENCE ENGINE is in debt to Laurie Anderson. Its title refers to Charles Babbage's mechanical engine for tabulating polynomial functions, a prototype for which was created in 1819 and completed in 1822.

PERNKOPF *ATLAS* refers to an anatomical atlas completed over a twenty-year period (1933–1953) by Austrian anatomist Eduard Pernkopf along with four artists. Pernkopf and the artists he employed were committed members of the Nazi Party and dissected prisoners of war and concentration camp inmates. Lines in italics come from Helmut Ferner's preface to the W. B. Saunders Company 1964 edition of the *Atlas*; and two works, Clara Leiser's *To and From the Guillotine* and a memorial stolperstein, which commemorate leaders of the German resistance group referred to as the Red Orchestra by the Gestapo. They were executed for their political activities. Some of their bodies were used in anatomical research.

ACKNOWLEDGMENTS

Many individuals and communities made this book imaginable, then possible. I owe uncountably infinite debts: to the team at Ecco, especially Daniel Halpern, Gabriella Doob, and Carolina Baizan, for the attentiveness and the opportunity; to my teachers; to the students of my teachers; to my first readers; to my always listeners; to my inspirers, conspirers, mentors, and guiders; to Nature, for not giving up on us just yet; to my family, forever. Thank you.

I am grateful to The Home School, the Artist Development Fund, the Edmond J. Safra Center for Ethics at Harvard, and the Frank Knox Memorial Fellowship for vital financial and institutional support.

Several poems rely on research conducted with the help, guidance, and participation of extraordinarily open-minded and generous people. I am especially appreciative of staff and affiliates of the following institutions: the Innocence Project; the Countway Library of Medicine; the Whipple Museum of the History of Science, of the Department of History and Philosophy of Science, University of Cambridge; the Huntsville Unit; and the Texas Prison Museum.

I am grateful to the editors of the venues in which these poems first appeared, sometimes in alternative forms:

Boston Review: "On Styrofoam"

Colorado Review: "Huttonian Theory of Earth"

Denver Quarterly: "War of the Currents"

Harper's Magazine: "1st Trial for the New Aubade"

Lana Turner: "Fragments from the Imagined Epic: *The Island of Stone Money*"

London Review of Books: "The Tamping Iron Speaks"

New Statesman: "Triple Witching," "How We Programmed the Apocalypse," "2nd Trial for the New Aubade"

New York Review of Books: "⏻ Trial for the New Aubade"

The New Yorker: "Objectivity as Blanket"

Paris Review: "Gesture Atlas," "Silent Auction" (as it appears here on page 11)

PEN America Poetry Series: "Division Day"

POETRY: "Stylized Facts"

Poets.org: "Pernkopf *Atlas* (I)" and "Pernkopf *Atlas* (II)"; "I Looked on My Right Hand and Beheld"

Sand Journal: "The Cryptographer Speaks"

Yale Review: "On Atrazine," "Proxy Means"